Exceptional
Entrepreneurship

Fast Track to Business Excellence

Other books in the series:

Mastering Change

Outstanding Leadership

Managing Your People

Exceptional Entrepreneurship

Real-Life Lessons from Top Business Leaders

Adapted from the Fifty Lessons
management collection

Published by BBC Books,
BBC Worldwide Limited,
Woodlands, 80 Wood Lane,
London W12 0TT

First published 2005
Copyright © Fifty Lessons, 2005

The moral right of the author has been asserted.

ISBN: 0563 51936 3

Commissioning Editor
Emma Shackleton
Editors for Fifty Lessons
Adam Sodowick and **Jenny Watts**
Editor
Sarah Sutton
Designer
Andrew Barron @ Thextension
Typesetter
Kevin O'Connor
Production Controller
Man Fai Lau

Set in Clarendon Light and Scala sans
Printed and bound in Great Britain by
Goodman Baylis

Contents

Acknowledgements

We would like to thank all of the executives who have contributed their hard-won lessons to the Fifty Lessons business library.

We believe that recording the first-hand learning experiences of today's business leaders will prove to be of immeasurable value to the business leaders of the future.

We'd also like to thank all those who have believed in, and contributed their time to, this growing and exciting initiative. Your support has been invaluable.

From the team at Fifty Lessons

About Fifty Lessons

Wherever you are on the career ladder, you are walking in the footsteps of others. Whatever business dilemma you are facing, some of the finest brains in business have faced it before.

Fifty Lessons was born out of a desire to learn from the experience of today's greatest business minds. We felt that decades of hard-won business experience were being written off to the vagaries of memory and resolved to capture, store and pass on this wisdom to the next generation.

Using the power of storytelling, we have captured on film the most valuable and defining experiences of some of the biggest names in international business, and built them into a digital library containing over 400 lessons.

The *Fast Track to Business Excellence* series features specially chosen lessons from this library, offering inspiration, practical help and guidance across a diverse range of management challenges. In business, as in life, learning from the knowledge of others is invaluable. We believe that there is no substitute for experience.

Adam Sodowick

Co-founder

For access to filmed interviews from the entire Fifty Lessons management collection, please visit: www.fiftylessons.com

Introduction to Exceptional Entrepreneurship

Every entrepreneur is driven by passion but not every entrepreneur is able to make a success of their idea. Self-belief, learning to overcome setbacks, the power of persuasion and sheer persistence all contribute massively to achieving this success.

Exceptional Entrepreneurship gives you access to the personal stories of ten entrepreneurial giants in a pocket-sized format. Their inspirational stories, and how they learnt from their experiences, will address the unique issues and obstacles that start-up businesses face, whilst showing you the qualities needed to make a business successful.

This entrepreneurial journey covers the passions and pitfalls of starting a new business, and the great value of storytelling in selling an idea. Successful entrepreneurs need unshakeable belief in their idea, combined with single-minded focus to gain backing and credibility in the marketplace. A potent mixture of luck, good partnerships and sound business instincts are also vital factors in an entrepreneur's success.

If you have a spark of entrepreneurial flame this book will provide you with the knowledge, insight and understanding necessary to fast track you to the next stage of development.

Entrepreneurs are anti-
hierarchical creative
people who are obsessed
with their business.
They are also a fountain
of ideas, but often need
others to help make
them happen.

1a   **The DNA of the Entrepreneur**
        Dame Anita Roddick

        Founder, *The Body Shop International*

My Career

"When I was in my twenties I worked at the *International Herald Tribune* in Paris and for the United Nations in the International Labor Office. In the 1960s I realized that travel was my 'university without walls', so I spent two or three years travelling, and that's where I got the original idea for the Body Shop. I had trained as a teacher, and so taught for a time on my return; then I met my husband, Gordon Roddick. We set up home and had an income from a *Fawlty Towers*-style hotel. I got bored with that, so although we kept it we opened a restaurant. My husband got bored with that and suggested we should go to Australia and open up a pineapple plantation. I said: 'Well, I've got this little idea for a body shop.' He thought that was a bit 'girly' for him and said: 'Well, you do that; I'm going to ride a horse from Buenos Aires to New York.' The kids were young at the time, so they weren't going to go with him and I can't ride a horse; so he went off riding for two years and I opened up the Body Shop. When he came back he said: 'Now, this looks interesting.' The rest is history.

Dame Anita Roddick

Founder, *The Body Shop International*

Entrepreneurship is as much about managing an obsession as it is about growing a business.

An entrepreneur has most in common with a crazy person. That's how I articulated it to myself when I began to realize that entrepreneurship is as much about managing an obsession as it is about growing a business: the link made sense to me. Entrepreneurship is obsessive and has certain core components, including a work ethic: that's why immigrants make terrific entrepreneurs – and that's why middle-aged, middle-class, wealthy and young people don't.

You've got to have an obsession with freedom to be an entrepreneur; you're almost unemployable and you therefore have to create your own skill base to overcome that. An entrepreneur cannot stand hierarchy – especially female entrepreneurs, who try to break it down at all times. I've learnt that you are tied by an umbilical cord to your business; you really don't know where life ends and where business begins. It all blurs together. I've also observed that when entrepreneurs leave their company they can often end up either needing mental health care or having suicidal feelings because their reason for being is their company.

The skills entrepreneurs need in their first few years are not the same as those they'll need later on. I learnt that really

The biggest lesson for me was to realize that I needed others to capture my ideas and make them happen: people who had all the skills I didn't have.

fast. The skill of an entrepreneur is to come up with great ideas. Like a genie in a bottle, we vomit ideas all the time. But unless there is somebody in the company who can expedite that skill – take an idea, catch it and then make it happen – the danger is that you're just vomiting ideas. I've had hundreds of ideas – creative, political, clothes-related – that have gone nowhere because I haven't found the right person to make them happen.

The biggest lesson for me was to realize that I needed others to capture my ideas and make them happen – people who had the skills I didn't have in areas such as finance: I wasn't interested in that side of things, and I needed somebody else to manage the figures. I needed somebody to handle processing, somebody to do purchasing... The skill is to keep hold of all the balloons: it's the best skill an entrepreneur can have. Let the business energy go the way the balloons want to go, but always hold the strings of the balloons very tightly together. For me, it was important to hold tightly to the values and creativity of the company.

The major lesson for an entrepreneur is never to go public: unless you want simply to sell your company. You can get everything you want if you just wait. Once you get into the stock market, you are in danger of being seduced by the new cultural imperative that everything of importance is connected to personal wealth. Business today isn't about job creation: it's about wealth creation for an ever-decreasing number of people – mostly the executive committee.

If you have the courage to stay as you are and tread water – and, if necessary, do things more slowly – you can keep your freedom. You can go below the radar screen of the media; you can be as experimental and as creative as you can imagine, and you can have more fun doing it.

The skill is to keep hold of all the balloons: it's the best skill an entrepreneur can have. Let the business energy go the way the balloons want to go, but always hold the strings of the balloons very tightly together.

Enthusiasm is an unstoppable force and the essential ingredient for starting a business successfully.

1b   **Enthusiasm**

Women are good at combining their interests with their skills and transforming them into a livelihood.

My early years in the Body Shop, some twenty-eight years ago, are now shrouded in the mists of time. The venture started as a livelihood; we don't use the word livelihood too much these days. But when the Body Shop started it wasn't a business — it wasn't arrogant enough to be a business. Women are good at combining their interests with their skills and transforming them into a livelihood. As a teacher, I was good at research. During my period of travel I lived with pre-industrial people and island communities, and I used everything they used to wash my hair, skin and body. When I decided to open the Body Shop I had about twenty great ideas to build on based on their natural products. Apart from those I had nothing; I knew nothing about financial theories or strategies.

I remember going to the bank to ask for £4000. We had collateral: our own little house and income from our hotel. I took our two kids with me; they were about three and five at the time. I was wearing a Bob Dylan T-shirt and jeans. Never go to the bank with enthusiasm. Bank managers are geared not to accept enthusiasm. They know how to prepare and protect money, but they really don't want to give too much of it away. I didn't measure up very well that day.

When enthusiasm comes from your heart it's unstoppable because it's driving your life and it's part of the template of who you are.

I returned to the bank looking like a man, dressed in a pinstriped suit with a profit-and-loss sheet – which was made up – in a plastic folder, and I got my £4000. Actually, *I* didn't. My husband got the £4000; I set about finding a little shop. The mistakes I made in the early days were out of an arrogance that stemmed from naivety. I didn't have any written materials; I didn't look for advice; I wasn't going to employ anyone from Harvard Business School: business graduates were too damn boring in my view. That attitude really came to haunt me later on. What worked for me and what drove me was enthusiasm. When enthusiasm comes from your heart it's unstoppable because it's driving your life and it's part of the template of who you are.

Stories are at the base of education and are an important form of communication. Highlighting the stories behind your products is a very powerful medium for engaging customers.

1c   The Power of the Story

The Power of the Story

During the early years of the Body Shop we were primarily a communications company; it just so happened we had some good products to enable us to earn a livelihood. We knew how to communicate: that was the essential ingredient that got us noticed. It was hard work and it was breathtakingly funny, especially since our first shop was stuck between two funeral parlours.

The funeral parlours objected to the name the Body Shop because coffins had to pass the shop a few times each day. I remember thinking: 'They cannot stop me using the name, but I can have fun out of this.' I made an anonymous phone call to the local paper with a handkerchief over the mouthpiece and told them I was a little woman setting up her first shop in Brighton: it was called the Body Shop and I was being intimidated by mafia undertakers. They thought: 'Our first sex shop, how exciting!' and ran a story. That was my first piece of free publicity. I never paid a penny for advertising. I knew that gaining press coverage was all about storytelling.

Storytelling provides the basis for communication around the world. When I travelled I found that it was at the base of education in most countries and in most societies. I knew that if I used the past as a prologue to introduce my products, then took the stories of the ingredients from the past and used them as a basis to explain what I was selling now, I would captivate my market. Storytelling was a major component of our success.

Storytelling provides the basis for communication around the world... Storytelling was a major component of our success.

I created stories in the press by being more interesting than others in the cosmetics industry, to which the press response was often: 'I can't believe you're saying this!' We produced a product called Honey Beeswax in Almond Oil. It was a cleanser that we made from beeswax from the hives in our garden. I remember noticing lots of black bits in the blend after filling twenty pots or so, and thought to myself: 'It's the dirty footprints of the bees from walking down the pathway.' I later said to the customers: 'Don't worry about the black bits in the cream; it's just the dirty footprints of the bees. Simply take them out with a spoon.' That style of communication had a grace because we didn't know you were allowed to tell lies: that you can is pretty outrageous when you think of the beauty business.

Then we discovered the power of visuals. Visuals are a vital element of communication. We learnt to communicate through a combination of graphic illustrations and the power of story – but, for us, stories were the most important form of communication.

Executive Timeline Dame Anita Roddick

1962–1976	***International Herald Tribune***, Paris
	Teacher of English and history, England
	International Labor Organization, United Nations, Geneva
	Hotel and restaurant, Littlehampton
	Owner and Manager, with Gordon Roddick
1976	**The Body Shop**
	Opened first branch in Brighton, Sussex. The Body Shop sells naturally inspired beauty products and is committed to environmental and social change.
1977	Gordon Roddick instigated the self-financing programme that sparked the growth of the franchise network.
1984	The Body Shop went public. Now a multi-local business with 1980 stores serving over 77 million customers in fifty different markets in twenty-five different languages and across twelve time zones.
2002	**Anita Roddick Publications**
	The publishing company established by Anita Roddick. Appointed Dame Commander of the British Empire (DBE).
2003	**Anita Roddick Books**
	www.anitaroddick.com
2004	**www.takeitpersonally.org**

The initial DNA of a company is very hard to change, so it is imperative to get it right from the outset. Choose your business partner carefully and consider what complementary skills they need to have, then work with them to set the tone of the company.

2a   **Select the Right Business Partner**
Brent Hoberman

Co-founder and Chief Executive, *lastminute.com*

My Career

I studied French and German literature at university, which helped me when lastminute.com expanded into Europe. After I graduated I went to a company called Mars & Co, a strategy consultancy from which I am proud to say I was fired after twenty months for being a prima donna. Just as I was being fired, I received a note on my desk to say that Spectrum Strategy had called me; they wanted to offer me a job. So I was fired on a Thursday with a week's pay in lieu of notice and started my new job the following Monday.

Spectrum Strategy was a media and telecom strategy consultancy that held much more interest for me. I did a lot of Internet work and then moved to LineOne, an Internet service provider. I spent six months there as a Business Development Executive, focusing on e-commerce, and then spent four months helping to start QXL, the European auction site. I started lastminute.com with Martha Lane Fox in 1998.

Brent Hoberman

Co-founder and Chief Executive, *lastminute.com*

Select the Right Business Partner

An early Board member of lastminute.com once said: 'One of the most important things to understand about business is that the initial DNA of a company is very hard to change: the first people you select to work with you set the DNA and the tone of the company, often forever, so you've got to get it right early on.' That meant hiring really smart, sparky people from the outset. The other important factor for me personally was to have a great business partner. Martha Lane Fox, my well-known co-founder, was an inspired choice and an immense influence.

> One of the most important things to understand about business is that the initial DNA of a company is very hard to change.

I was the tenth employee at Spectrum Strategy, Martha was the eleventh – and she wouldn't have been the eleventh if I'd had my way. I was a very junior employee at the time I interviewed her. I was unsure about her because she didn't want to do the 'geeky' computer modelling that I wanted somebody to take away from me. Fortunately, the other people interviewing her were smart enough to say: 'Actually, she's pretty good, so we'll take her anyway.' We worked together for a couple of years at Spectrum Strategy before we each went our separate ways. Martha went to Carlton and I went on to do some Internet jobs.

Sharing the same vision and being motivated by the same goal was very important... When it came to business we could finish each other's sentences.

I approached Martha as my second choice for lastminute.com after the person I had discussed the idea with initially said he didn't want to do it. I said: 'Why don't you come and do this because surely working at Carlton can't be as much fun?' Fortunately, she wasn't wild about Carlton, but then she wasn't actually wild about the Internet either at the time, or about lastminute.com as an idea. She had to be persuaded – and fortunately she *was* persuaded – and we started working together.

One of the things that made lastminute.com work so well was that the two of us enjoyed working together. Our motivation wasn't solely to make money: that was the side product. We wanted to build a service that was useful, and we were motivated by the satisfaction of building something. Sharing the same vision and being motivated by the same goal was very important; having complementary skills was great as well. Martha and I came at things from different perspectives but shared the same vision. When it came to business we could finish each other's sentences, which in meetings is a great and rare quality.

When deciding whom to go into business with, or whether a partnership might be successful, the first consideration must be whether or not you get on with that person: do you trust him or her implicitly? There are some business partnerships that work very well, even though the people don't enjoy working together. Personally, I think life's too short for that. We all spend so much time working that it's important to ensure the people around you are people you enjoy working with, whom you have fun with and who have good energy. In addition, nobody's good at everything, so selecting a business partner also requires an understanding of the complementary skills the person might have. Fortunately, Martha and I are good at different things, so that worked quite well for us.

There are some business partnerships that work very well, even though the people don't enjoy working together. Personally, I think life's too short for that.

The initial team and the partners you choose will set the cultural tone of the company, probably forever. It's therefore very important, particularly in businesses that are founder-driven, that their culture is right – which means ensuring that everybody in the business is focused on the right issues.

One of the greatest challenges for small companies starting up is creating a credible name for themselves. Having people with proven business cachet advising you is one way of achieving this, and attracting established brands early helps the business punch above its weight.

2b   **Establish Credibility Early**

Establish Credibility Early

One of the greatest challenges for a small start-up company is how to gain credibility because anyone dealing with your company will be worried, obviously, that you might go out of business. There are many things that can be done to tackle this. The most obvious is to raise money by not being afraid to give away equity. Retaining some of the equity is important, but you need to ask yourself: 'What is the bigger picture? What's my probability of success? If I give away a bit of equity now, am I going to have a slightly smaller part of something much larger in the long run?' The other thing you can do is to gather great people around you: highly credible people who have good experience.

Having spent ten months working in the Internet industry before I started lastminute.com, I was able to get good people for the team. They were highly respected Board members who had run big companies such as Intercontinental and KLM, and were valuable even though they were figureheads rather than active participants in the day-to-day business. Peter Bouw, the former Chairman of KLM, was a major national player, who gave us a lot of credibility with the airlines. The airline companies were amongst the hardest to get on board because they were very worried about upsetting the travel industry and travel agents: we were the smallest player in the market, yet they were to supply us with the best deals, which created an interesting situation.

The challenge at the beginning was about how to get the first supplier when we had no suppliers at all.

None of the companies involved wanted to be the first to be named publicly. We therefore focused on getting four big names on board, so we could say: 'We've got Lufthansa, Alitalia, BMI, KLM, etc.' Getting them all together was important. Hotel chains, such as the Savoy Group, were much more concerned about the company they would be keeping on our website; in that instance it was important that we could show them that their product would not be presented as part of a bucket shop deal, but would be featured alongside other quality products and brands. The challenge at the beginning was very much about how to get the first supplier when we had no suppliers at all. Once the first few were on board, it became possible to tell the others: 'You'll be featured alongside other quality names.' Then they felt comfortable.

After winning some brand names the next hurdle became investment. We raised about £600,000 in the early days. One of the first-round investors was Inovacom, which was part of France Telecom. It was a great advantage to be able then to tell people that we had their backing. In the next round we got Intel and Deutsche Telecom on board, and gradually we built a groundswell of support. The response suddenly became: 'This isn't a small venture; this is backed by Deutsche Telecom, France Telecom and Intel.' If you've got smart people backing you, you have instant credibility, so we got brand name venture capitalists behind us.

The final challenge relates to the partners you're working with. When we went live our homepage featured a selection of the top ten brand names in the business. In turn, lastminute.com was on their homepages or on their sites: they were linking to us and we could use their name on our site, which gave us further credibility. When you're really small it is useful to make the business seem bigger than it is. When you number just ten people in a back office it's important to give credibility and gravitas to the business to ensure that the people who work with you and for you realize you're serious.

We weren't just putting a flag in the ground and saying: 'Here's a nice idea, why doesn't someone else do it properly?' We wanted to convey the impression, right from day one, that this was a great idea and that there was no point in anybody else copying us because we were going to do it really, really well. We let it be known that we had a huge level of backing and enormous support, so any prospective competitors should just leave the market space to us.

Executive Timeline Brent Hoberman

Early career	**Mars & Co**
	Graduate Trainee
	Mars & Co is a strategy consultancy.
	Spectrum Strategy Consultants
	Senior Associate
	Spectrum worked in media and telecoms.
	LineOne
	Business Development Executive
	Acquired five years of strategic consultancy experience at this Internet service provider owned by News International, British Telecom and United News & Media.
	QXL
	Founding member and Head of Business Development
	Helped found this European auction site.
April 1998	**lastminute.com**
	Co-founder and Chief Executive Officer
	lastminute.com is an independent travel and leisure website co-founded with Martha Lane Fox.
2000	*Executive Director*
2002	Bought UK travel services provider Travelselect.com and the Destination Holdings Group (DGL).
2003	Acquired Med Hotels.
2004	Acquired the lastminute.de group of companies in Germany.

The motivation
to launch a new
business often stems
from an individual's
dissatisfaction with
an existing product
or service. The
most successful
entrepreneurial ideas
can transform an
existing idea into
something that is both
different and better.

3a   **Changing the Marketplace**
      Karan Bilimoria

Founder and Chief Executive Officer, *Cobra Beer*

My Career

I was born and brought up in India, and went to university at the age of sixteen, having skipped my A levels. I graduated aged nineteen with a degree in commerce, but far too young to have learnt anything of consequence. I came to the UK the same year and qualified as a Chartered Accountant with Ernst & Young in London. During my training I realized that I wasn't going to be an accountant for the rest of my life, but I still valued the qualification and the training I was receiving. On the day that I qualified I left Ernst & Young and went to Cambridge University to take a law degree. I had an amazing time at Cambridge, and came up with my idea for Cobra Beer while a student there.

I started in business within six months of graduating. I had captained the Cambridge University polo team on its first tour of India and had returned with some sample polo sticks that the makers had asked me to sell on their behalf. I sold them to Harrods and Lillywhites, and from that moment I was in business. I teamed up with my friend Arjun Reddy, and in early 1989 the two of us started importing a variety of goods from India: high-fashion items, leather and silk goods, polo sticks and various other products.

We started working on Cobra Beer in September 1989, and the first container of it arrived in June of the following year. We stopped all our other business projects once the beer business started to develop because Cobra was the 'Big Idea' and we wanted to focus on building the brand. My business partner left the company in 1995. Since then, I have built a team and together we have brought Cobra Beer to where it is today, and will drive its growth in the future.

I believe very strongly in lifelong learning, and began attending courses such as the Business Growth Programme at Cranfield Business School. I regularly attend a course at the Harvard Business School and the London Business School. I advocate ongoing training for everyone throughout my company, and I bring in outside trainers from around the world and encourage people to attend courses. I want everyone to be as outward-looking as possible, and to engage in activities outside the business.

I sit on a number of government boards, and am involved with some charities, including the Loomba Trust, which educates the children of poor widows in India, and Welfare to Work.

Karan Bilimoria

Founder and Chief Executive Officer, *Cobra Beer*

Changing the Marketplace

The majority of business ideas aren't brand new: they are not inventions or products that never existed before. Invariably, the ideas develop because people are dissatisfied with an existing product or service and think: 'I can do this better, I can do this differently, I can change the marketplace.' My own idea, Cobra Beer, developed while I was a student in the UK. I used to eat Indian food regularly at restaurants and when you eat spicy food you feel thirsty and you want to drink something cold and refreshing; that's why over two-thirds of people in Indian restaurants drink lager.

I did not like the lagers that were available in this country. I found them too fizzy; they caused bloating, particularly with Indian food. An English friend introduced me to real ale (English bitter), which I love to this day, but it didn't take me long to discover that ale and Indian food just don't go together. That's where my idea for Cobra Beer came from: it evolved from the realization that the restaurant owner could be selling me more food and more beer. I envisaged that one day I would be bringing my own beer from India, a lager beer that

My idea was simple: most business ideas *are* very simple, but of course the challenge is to make the idea happen.

would be refreshing, less gassy and smoother than European lager, that would accompany Indian food and also appeal to ale drinkers. It was a simple idea: most business ideas *are* very simple, but of course the challenge is to make the idea happen. You would have thought that the beer industry, which is thousands of years old, would have come up with a similar lager in the past, but no one had. That's the amazing thing: whenever a successful business idea is launched that is impressive in its simplicity, the natural response is: 'Why didn't somebody think of that before?'

When you come up with a sound idea you need to take a leap and start the business. There is no short cut. Once you have done that, the next step is to cross the credibility gap.

When you come up with a sound idea you need to take a leap and start the business. There is no short cut. You've got to make the commitment and go for it. Once you have done that, the next step is to cross the credibility gap – that space in the market where nobody knows you or your product, but you've got to get people to supply you, to finance you and to buy from you. They're only going to want to do that if you have confidence, faith and passion in your product and idea. Your personal qualities give them the confidence to give you a chance.

There are lots of examples of entrepreneurs being different and producing better products. For example, James Dyson didn't *invent* the vacuum cleaner, he came up with a better way of *producing* a vacuum cleaner: a way that has changed the marketplace forever, to the extent that manufacturers of traditional cleaners are now producing models based on the cleaners that Dyson developed.

People will only want to supply you, finance you and buy from you if you have confidence, faith and passion in your product and idea.

Richard Branson didn't invent airlines, but he found in-flight service very boring, so he came up with a way of making flying much more fun and interesting. His approach has changed the face of airline travel, and now all airlines are paying more attention to in-flight entertainment and service.

One individual can change the marketplace forever – whether with a service or a product – by coming up with something that's both different and better.

These examples show ways in which one individual can change the marketplace forever – whether with a service or a product – by coming up with something that's both different and better.

Create a product that is different and better that will change the marketplace forever. Maintain faith in your idea at all times; in the early days people will tell you: 'It can't be done,' but don't listen to detractors. Be persistent and always believe you have the right product, as your self-belief will win through in the end.

Having Faith in Your Idea

When you come up with an entrepreneurial idea for a new business or product, invariably it's going to be against all odds because you're starting from nothing and you've got to create something and make it a success in an environment that is usually very competitive. In the case of Cobra, our vision was to produce a new beer and launch it in Britain — the most competitive beer market in the world. Looking back, those early days were incredibly hard: early progress involved a lot of sacrifice, a huge number of hours worked and a great deal of frustration.

I remember how it felt to know we had the right product, to know our idea was special.

I remember how it felt to *know* we had the right product, to *know* our idea was special: in our case, we were producing a less gassy, extra-smooth lager that complemented all cuisines and appealed to both ale drinkers and lager drinkers alike. We had proof it was working because we were getting regular repeat orders from our customers, we were achieving new sales and the product was being well accepted. Making progress was still a hard, hard slog: it felt as if we were a jet aircraft fully laden with fuel, zooming down the runway but unable to lift off the ground. Of course, eventually, it did; there was some intermittent turbulence and then we were on our way up.

I had pennies, literally just pennies, in my wallet. Did I feel down in the dumps at those times? You bet I did. But did I think of giving up? Absolutely never.

There were times during that period when we completely ran out of money. I remember sitting at our office table, which was a dining table in a loft conversion in Fulham, and looking in my wallet: every credit card was up to its limit, every one of our bank accounts was well over the limit; I had pennies, literally just pennies, in my wallet. Did I feel down in the dumps at those times? You bet I did. But did I think of giving up? Absolutely never.

I'll never forget my first meeting at the brewery in India. I'd flown in and was taken to meet the management team of the largest independent brewery in the country. They were hugely successful. There in a semi-circle sat the brewery's entire management team: the Company Secretary, the Chief Accountant, the General Manager, the Head Brewer, the Vice President of Marketing, the Managing Director, all in a big semi-circle; I'd never met any of them before. Every single one of them, individually and collectively, laughed in my face and said: 'You don't stand a chance; none of our competitors has succeeded except one; what makes you think you're going

There in a semi-circle sat the brewery's management team... Every single one of them, individually and collectively, laughed in my face.

to succeed?' I told them: 'I am going to succeed because I have faith in my idea and I know my product is going to be different; it is going to be better than the competition and we're going to create the best Indian beer that's ever been brewed and to make it a global beer brand. I need your support and I need you to work with me to make that happen.' Fortunately, they decided to help.

If you have faith that you can make something happen, you can put up with everything along the way, as long as that long-term goal is in place and as long as you believe you're going to make it to your destination. If you have that belief, you will find a way to overcome the obstacles and the hardships. If you have faith in your idea, if you have confidence, then go for it. Our vision and motto at Cobra is to 'aspire and achieve against all odds, with integrity'.

Creating an atmosphere of trust, respect and flexibility enables ideas and motivation to flourish, resulting in rapid growth and constant new product development.

3c   Succeeding Against the Giants

Speed gives us the advantage. We can come up with a new product idea and implement development from start to finish in a matter of months, where a corporate giant would probably take years.

A small, new company with a new brand *can* succeed against the giants, provided it has the ability to come up with ideas and put them into action very, very quickly. To achieve that takes entrepreneurial spirit – a quality that has to be present within every member of the team, not just the entrepreneurial leader; it has to feature across the company in every way. It is important to create an environment where the spirit of entrepreneurship can flourish.

In 2004 we were ranked in the *Sunday Times* 'Best 50 SMEs (Small-to-Medium Enterprises) to Work For'. I am extremely proud of my team for having made that list. One of the categories in which we were judged top was 'enabling people to be in control of their own work'. I believe that it is absolutely crucial for people to feel in control of their own work because it means they will also feel they have the flexibility and ability to come up with ideas, they will want to put those ideas into action, and they will want to get fast results. Speed gives us the advantage. We can come up with a new product idea and implement development from start to finish in a matter of months, where a corporate giant would probably take years. The creation of an entrepreneurial environment has to involve the business leaders 'letting go' in order to show trust and respect for the talents of other people. In granting individuals flexibility and respect we are also implying that we trust them. That trust is returned in the form of respect and trust for the company, for the brand and for the management team; it is not necessarily about demanding respect or even earning it – it is about giving it. Letting go is about taking calculated risks; it is about management allowing people to get on with things. What develops as a result is an atmosphere where there's a buzz, and there's an amazing buzz across Cobra Beer. In an atmosphere where there is a lot of excitement it is good to get everyone engaged in developing new ideas, not just the department that's dealing with new product development.

The result of creating an atmosphere in which people are encouraged to come up with ideas is that no one is scared they will be ridiculed for trying to contribute. At worst their

The creation of an entrepreneurial environment has to involve the business leaders 'letting go' in order to trust and respect the talents of other people... It is about management allowing people to get on with things.

The key to maintaining our competitive edge is to nurture an entrepreneurial spirit.

idea won't go ahead, but praise is given where praise is due. In such an environment, if things aren't going well, people will know that too. It is crucial that people know where they stand.

We try to encourage this openness in a number of ways: for example, we invite submissions for 'Ideas of the Month'. People from all across the company are encouraged to put their thought into the ideas box (it's not a suggestions box), and at the end of each month a member of the company is selected, or volunteers are invited, to choose the top three 'Ideas of the Month'. Those chosen are not necessarily from management; they can be from any part of the company. On the last Friday of the month we all gather round, the ideas are announced and prizes are given. These are wonderful ideas that come from all areas of the company.

The key to maintaining our competitive edge is to nurture an entrepreneurial spirit. Our environment of continual, fast-moving, entrepreneurial innovation will always give us the edge over the business giants.

Executive Timeline Karan Bilimoria

1982–1986	**Ernst & Young** *Trainee Chartered Accountant* Worked in audit, tax, training and accounting.
1988	Degree in law, Cambridge University
1988	**Cresvale Ltd**, London (part of S. & W. Beresford) *Consulting Accountant*
1989	**European Accounting Focus** *Sales and Marketing Director*
1989	**Cobra Beer** *Founder and Chief Executive Officer* The brand has a current retail value turnover approaching £65 million, is sold in over 6000 Indian restaurants, 5000 bars, pubs and clubs, and in thousands of supermarket and off-licence outlets. Cobra Beer is exported to more than thirty countries worldwide and operates international subsidiaries on three continents.
1999	**General Bilimoria Wines** Launched premium house wine range now served in hundreds of Indian restaurants, including London's Michelin-starred restaurants.

> Never underestimate the power of luck in helping to build global businesses.

4 **Luck**
   Sir Martin Sorrell

   Group Chief Executive, *WPP*

My Career

I was born in 1945 and went to Haberdashers' Aske's School in a Jewish community in northwest London. I was granted a place at Cambridge University, but before I went there I had a summer job at the journal *Management Today*, so I'm a frustrated journalist really. At Cambridge I read economics.

I went straight to Harvard Business School after that and had a summer job in the UK at Marks & Spencer. After graduating from Harvard in 1969 I worked for Glendenning Associates – a marketing consultancy in Westport, Connecticut. Then I joined Mark McCormack at IMG – the sports and lifestyle marketing and management company. At the time they managed Arnold Palmer, Gary Player, Jack Nicklaus, Jean-Claude Killy, Jean Shrimpton – the light of my life – and all sorts of other interesting people.

After that I joined James Gulliver of the Argyll Group as a Personal Financial Advisor, which meant that I carried his bags and was his gofer. He made an investment in Saatchi & Saatchi: I met Maurice and Charles Saatchi and became their Chief Financial Officer for nine years. Following my attack of andropause in 1985, I decided to go into business for myself – hence WPP. I'm Chief Executive of WPP, one of the world's largest communications services companies, and it's a job I've been enjoying for twenty years.

Sir Martin Sorrell

Group Chief Executive, *WPP*

Luck

Being in the right place at the right time is critically important in business, as it is in life.

Luck is terribly important. It may sound a little demeaning to say so, but I believe it played a very important role in the starting of WPP.

About twenty years ago I was the Chief Finance Officer at Saatchi & Saatchi and had been doing the job for about nine years. I was forty years old and I wanted to start my own business. I teamed up with a stockbroker partner and we went looking for a shell company. We wanted to find a small public company that was listed, and preferably in manufacturing so that we could move into the service area.

We alighted on a company called Wire & Plastic Products, which is where the WPP name subsequently originated. One of the plastic products came from a small, Kent-based manufacturing company and wireworks near Dartford, with about £3 million of sales and £300,000 of profits. Luck was an important contributing factor because in these shell games establishing trust with the incumbent management is terribly important, given that we said we were going to come in and revolutionize the company.

The head of the company was Gordon Sampson. He invited us to travel down to Dartford for a two o'clock meeting – pointedly not for lunch! We were desperately hungry, so we went into a fish and chip shop near the wireworks and bought ourselves a bag of chips to eat in the car before we went into the meeting. We must have been stinking of vinegar when we arrived, and I think Gordon thought we did it for effect to prove we were men of the people.

We talked to Gordon for about an hour. He was intrigued and called his stockbrokers – a company called Panmure Gordon, which is part of Lazard & Co Ltd LLC. He spoke to a Senior Partner or Partner at Panmure Gordon, a company that I'd known for many years, and the Partner said to Gordon: 'Well, Sorrell knows what he's doing.' That was piece of luck number one.

Gordon Sampson's other advisor was County Bank, which was also advisor to Saatchi & Saatchi, where I'd been the CFO. Gordon picked up the phone to his Account Officer at County Bank and said: 'We've met this fellow Martin Sorrell, and we don't know him. What's he like?' To which the County Bank advisor said: 'This is very difficult for us; there's a conflict of interest here because we advise Saatchis and we also advise you. Let me think about it for a few hours; I'll come back to you tomorrow morning.'

He called back in the morning and said: 'I really can't say anything but, off the record, let me tell you a story. There was a man called Greg Hutchins at Tompkins, who used to work for Hansen. Greg Hutchins went to Tompkins and bought a stake in the company. The share price on the day before he bought the stake was 10p, and by the end of the first day's trading – after the announcement of the techno stake in the company – it was 60p. That's all I'm going to say. I'll just leave it at that.' Gordon put down the phone and that was the story.

Luck, in the sense of being in the right place at the right time, is critically important in business, as it is in life. Life is a series of circles, and as long as you pursue a lot of the circles – people these days call it networking – and provided you establish contacts, connections or a reputation that reverberates around an industry or industries, that will hold you in good stead. Ultimately, however, luck plays a very important part. If we'd gone to a company where there were no connections with advisors, the deal probably wouldn't have happened. **"**

Executive Timeline Sir Martin Sorrell

	Graduated – Cambridge University
1968	Graduated – Harvard Business School
1968–69	**Glendenning Associates**, Westport, CT
	A US-based marketing consultancy
1970–74	**Mark McCormack Organization**
	Managing the business affairs of sports personalities
1975–1977	**James Gulliver Associates**
	Working personally for James Gulliver.
1977–1984	**Saatchi & Saatchi plc**
	Group Finance Director
	The advertising agency group
1986	**WPP**
	Group Chief Executive
	One of the world's largest communications services companies.
	Major brands include advertising agencies: JWT Company, Ogilvy & Mather Worldwide and Y&R.

There are many pitfalls to starting a new business. Keep focused, don't fall in love with the product, don't try to develop another business alongside your day job, and remember that it will always cost much more than you anticipate.

5a

The Pitfalls of Starting a Business
Sir Mark Weinberg

President, St James's Place Capital

My Career

 I trained and worked originally as a lawyer, but in 1961 I went into business to form Abbey Life Assurance. I worked and built up that company for about eight years, and in 1970 it was bought out by ITT. The circumstances were such that I lost confidence in the shareholders, so I left. In 1971 I started a new company, originally called Hambro Life, but we changed its name subsequently to Allied Dunbar. This company was bought by BAT Industries in the mid-1980s, and in 1990 I left to start a new company called St James's Place.

Sir Mark Weinberg

President, *St James's Place Capital*

The Pitfalls of Starting a Business

My belief, based upon experience, is that focus is probably
the most important factor in business. I believe in the need
for focus because when I've ignored it I've always regretted
it. A clear example of this took place in the early 1980s when
I was Chief Executive of Allied Dunbar Assurance Group,
which was very successful at the time. I had been feeling that
I had some time and a bit of money to spare when someone
came to me with a prototype of the first PDA (Personal Digital
Assistant). It was at about the time when the Psion organizer
was being developed, which became a great success. The PDA
I looked at was produced just before the Psion, and was a
better product than the Psion. It remained a better product for
quite a number of years, but there were three problems:

1) I fell in love with the product, which is something you
   should never do.
2) It was a pioneering product, which presented its own
   challenges.
3) I was handling this project on the side of my other work.
   I lost my focus.

My job running a life assurance company was a full-time
occupation, but I found time in the evenings, at weekends,
on the odd morning on the way to work, to go off to a factory
and get involved in running a start-up, high-tech business.
Ultimately, the business was not successful, and it cost me
quite a lot of money. Probably the only way I'll ever get that
money back will be by writing a book listing all the lessons
I learnt from the experience!

I had the 'missionary problem' because it was not just a case of marketing the value of my particular product – I had to market the *concept* as well.

Lesson number one is to be very careful about being a pioneer in business. The PDA idea was exciting because it was a totally new concept: a battery-driven computer that you could carry in your pocket and use to organize your life, write your diary, and draft your letters and faxes (there was no email at that time). At the outset, development was very exciting, but because it was a pioneering idea it took many years to catch on. Twenty years later, there are millions of similar products around: today's Palm Pilot, for example, is really a derivative of that prototype. Now people buy them, but in those days we battled to sell the first few, and couldn't understand why people shouldn't want them. So the first lesson is: be careful about being a pioneer.

The second lesson is never to fall in love with technology; in fact, never fall in love with a product at all. After six months or a year of work it became clear that making the business successful was going to be a very hard slog. That's when I began to be aware of the pioneering problem. I spoke to somebody at Olivetti who was in charge of technology development, and he used a phrase that has stayed with me.

My approach wasn't working and I should have cut the development much earlier, but I persevered because I'd fallen in love with the product.

He said I had the 'missionary problem' because it was not just a case of marketing the value of my particular product – I had to market the *concept* as well.

Three-quarters of my marketing spend had to go towards educating the public about the value of the new product. By contrast, for those competitors who followed, the marketing angle when selling a Psion or a palm product could be quite simply 'my product's better than their product' because by then people knew and understood the concept. My approach wasn't working, and I should have cut the development much earlier, but I persevered because I'd fallen in love with the product.

The third lesson is that I created another problem in trying to develop a pioneering product on the side, by myself. If you get involved in something, or want to finance a new concept – especially something outside your own field – go and find a really good person to run the company. Invest some of the money that would be sunk into building the business unsuccessfully into taking on somebody who can really build it up: who can live it, who can take it home, who can work on it during the day as well as the weekends. I tried to build it on the side. I thought: 'If I'm running a successful life company, I can do this as well,' but I couldn't. It's possible that if I had given up the life assurance company I would have made a success of the project, but even then it would still not have been a field I was experienced in.

If you get involved in something outside your own field, go and find a really good person to run the company.

An important lesson to learn on the financial side is that a new product, especially a pioneering product, will always cost a lot more than you think it's going to. In any business plan you put in a contingency. The usual approach, if you're playing it really safe, is to put in 10–20 per cent for contingency. When you are creating and marketing a pioneering product that contingency figure should be 100–200 per cent. Something unexpected will need to be paid for and you will need a lot more money. It will always cost more than you think it's going to. Something *always* goes wrong.

Never make the mistake of thinking that if you've invented something clever or brought something new into the marketplace, it will sell itself. It won't. The American poet and philosopher Ralph Waldo Emerson is often quoted as saying: 'Invent a better mousetrap and the world will beat a path to your door.' In reality, the world doesn't. Always set aside a big budget for marketing your product – probably a bigger budget than you would allocate for manufacturing. You've got to invent a better mousetrap and then spend a lot of money marketing it in order to make it a success.

Successfully marketing a new product does not require reinventing the wheel: it means presenting what you have in a better and more relevant way. Keep literature simple and don't overestimate the customer's understanding of, or interest in, what you are offering.

5b   **Successfully Marketing New Products**

I found a means of simplifying the product and of marketing it in a way that the public could understand.

I'd like to share my experience of innovation. I tend to be known in the life assurance industry as the person who first created unit-linked assurance thirty or forty years ago – which has now become the mainstay of the industry. The fact is that I wasn't its inventor: at the time I came into the market there were already five or six companies in the field. My approach was different because I found a means of simplifying the product and of marketing it in a way that the public could understand. It was marketed so successfully that we grew eventually to become the major force in the market. Most of the people who developed it originally didn't succeed with their products at all.

What I learnt from that experience is that you should think very carefully about being a pioneer in business. There's a saying in American books and marketing that pioneers get scalped; it's the colonists who follow afterwards who reap the rewards. In effect, this is what happened in unit-linked assurance because the original pioneers produced products that were overcomplicated and that people couldn't understand. In learning from their experience, we were able to be much more successful.

It's very easy to get overexcited about something you've developed personally, and to overestimate the ability of the public – your potential customers – to understand the product or service. This is especially true when selling an abstract concept, such as financial services: it is easy for the producer to get lost in jargon and become immersed in a concept that the public doesn't understand.

Pioneers get scalped; it's the colonists who follow afterwards who reap the rewards.

In the case of unit-linked assurance, the first thing I did was to produce literature that the public *could* understand. I found I have a facility for this. As I write a passage, I'm thinking as if I'm a member of the public: I'm hearing from inside the mind of the reader what I'm writing down. In that way I don't get lost in technical jargon and I remember that the person reading may have no knowledge of the product. I also assume that the reader is not necessarily that interested in the product. I've always worked on the theory that people want to stop reading at the end of every sentence they're reading. Based on that assumption, every sentence written needs not only to convey information, but also to entice people to read the next line as well.

My first priority was to produce literature in a form that the public would understand; the second was to ensure that the sales people were able to sell the message. If you're selling something abstract, people won't pick up the story for themselves, even if they are provided with a relatively well-written piece of literature. The literature provides a base on which to train salesmen to sell the product effectively: to sell the concept and then use the literature to back it up and reinforce the sale.

If sales are a bit slow, don't make the mistake of thinking: 'I must come up with a new product.' Don't assume that a new product will change the world. It won't. Be careful in particular of developing any kind of product based mainly upon it being a clever idea. Always start from the customer's side of the fence and ask: 'Is there a need that I can develop a product to fulfil?' Innovation isn't usually about thinking up a brand new idea. A successful innovation generally develops incrementally: it's about presenting a product in a better way, often by adding a new idea or by finding a better way of explaining the original concept. Being innovative is about creating a product or service that may be fundamentally the same as something that has existed previously, but that has been made more marketable, easier for people to understand, and that people feel is more relevant to their lives. Successful innovation often relates more to marketing than changes to the product itself.

Executive Timeline Sir Mark Weinberg

1961	**Abbey Life Assurance Company**
	Founding Director
	Founded Abbey Life Assurance Company in London, and formed one of the UK's first property funds.
1971	**Hambro Life Assurance** (now part of Zurich Financial Services)
	Founding Director
	Formed the first retail-managed fund.
	Grew to become the largest unit-linked life assurance company in the UK. Later renamed Allied Dunbar.
1985–1990	**Securities and Investment Board**
	Deputy Chairman
	Held role from the Board's inception in 1985. It was the principal UK regulatory body.
1991	**St James's Place Capital plc**
	Co-founder and Chairman
	St James's Place is a wealth management group.
2004	*President*

In business you learn from your failures. It's important to recognize, particularly early on in your career, that you're going to make mistakes. Early lessons are often hard-won, but will stand you in good stead during the course of your career.

6a **Learning from a Failure**
Michael Jackson

Chairman, *The Sage Group,* and Chairman, *Elderstreet*

My Career

I went to Cambridge University to study law. I then spent four years becoming an accountant. They were very tough years but they weren't wasted. After qualifying I went into industry, which was both fun and interesting, and then spent time in marketing for American companies. I realized after a few years that although it was quite good experience, I was never going to make any real money, so I wrote off to twenty venture capital firms and ended up working for a very small investment bank that went public in 1987 – a boom year. In 1990, when the market was a lot tougher, the founding Chairman of the company died. I lost out in a career fight for the role of CEO, so I was effectively forced out. In the same year I started Elderstreet, a mainly technology-based venture capital firm investing in the software sector. I sold the company to Dresdner Kleinwort Capital in 2000, then with a number of colleagues bought it back in 2003.

In parallel with that activity I had an interest in Sage, the business software company. I had been an investor in Sage in 1983 when there were three people in the business. In 1990 Sage became a public company. I was Deputy Chairman in 1993–4, and then became Chairman after the founding Chairman David Goldman stepped down and subsequently died. So I've been Chairman of Sage for the last seven years, but involved with the company for the last twenty-one. It has been a lot of fun seeing it grow. I currently sit as Chairman on the Board of seven or eight small public companies in addition to Sage and Elderstreet.

Michael Jackson

Chairman, *The Sage Group*, and Chairman, *Elderstreet*

Learning from a Failure

I didn't start from zero; I started from minus one or two – not a great place to begin, particularly when you're on your own and you're starting up a business.

In business you have to learn from your failures. It's important to recognize, particularly early on, that you're going to make mistakes. Some of those mistakes can be immensely beneficial in the long term.

My first syndicated investment was a Manchester-based company that specialized in typesetting. At that time typesetting was being affected by the introduction of digital technology, but I managed to convince myself that it was okay in this instance because the company was at the top end of its market and it would take a long time for the technology to have an impact. The net result was that within six months I had raised money from all my friends – my best friends – and had convened a great Board. I used up all the goodwill I had accumulated in business over ten years and then the company went bust – spectacularly bust. It was a horrible feeling. This was my first deal, completed over the course of six or seven months, and the signature tune for my new company. It was an absolute, unmitigated disaster.

As a result, I didn't start from zero; I started from minus one or two – not a great place to begin, particularly when you're on your own and you're starting up a business. I look back on events now and say that the outcome was a fantastic piece of luck in one sense because, had the investment been a big success, I would have gone on investing, thinking it was easy, and without having learned from some of my mistakes.

My first lesson is: if a company is in a state of flux, try to make sure that you are located near by. Travelling to Manchester every day, every other day, or every week just wasn't enough. I should either have lived there for a time and managed the business day to day, or I should have said: 'I'm not going to invest in a relatively immature business.' We had bought the business from receivership. It had some management problems and a number of issues that needed to be addressed, but it was a cheap buy, or so it appeared on the surface. However, it was a business in flux and it was geographically too far away from my home base.

If a company is in a state of flux, try to make sure that you are located near by.

The second lesson I learned is that if the wrong Managing Director or the wrong management is in place, don't mess around. If change is needed, make it very early on, particularly in early-stage small businesses because they're fragile: they don't have the luxury of being able to spend time waiting for things to happen. If intuition tells you that you've got the wrong

If a business can't afford to have a full-time Finance Director, don't start the business.

person in place, you must act. You can't say: 'Oh, it'll be all right.' You may want to believe that the guy's a good person because you appointed him or her and put your trust in them, but you can't do that. You've got to be dispassionate.

The third lesson relates to finance. There was a constant plea from the Managing Director that the company couldn't afford a full-time Finance Director. Big mistake. If a business – any business, of whatever size – can't afford to have a full-time Finance Director, don't start the business. If you don't know the numbers or you don't know whether they are right, it becomes like flying a plane in cloud with no instruments: you don't know where you are and you don't know where the problems are. In this particular case you can bet your bottom dollar that the Managing Director put an optimistic skew on things. I wouldn't say he deliberately hid things but he was battling to make sure the business stayed afloat. The reality was that he made them worse.

Those were my first lessons. They were hard-fought and have stood me in good stead over the years because the company failure was a massive embarrassment, and financially it was very bad news. I've applied those lessons many times since, both in relation to businesses that I haven't invested in and to businesses I have.

Entrepreneurial flair when combined with effective marketing skill is a rare and powerful combination in business. Developing products that customers want and being bold with marketing investment are vital factors in achieving long-term success.

6b **Entrepreneurial Marketing**

Entrepreneurial Marketing

At the heart of Sage's success is a man with great marketing skills, as well as great entrepreneurial ability. Such a combination is a very rare occurrence, particularly in the technology sector. The Sage story has been told before, but it describes such a huge success it is worth telling again. It is the story of David Goldman, a guy who had a printing works in Newcastle, who took on a Visiting Professor to do some technology work for him under a Department of Trade and Industry scheme.

The professor's brief was to create a software-based costing and estimating package for the printing industry. As anyone in the printing industry will realize, to cost and estimate a print job is a complex process: there can be any number of different colours, lengths and other criteria involved. Sage produced the product, then started to sell it, and subsequently produced an accounting product. I raised venture capital for them and, as is my style, I invested my fee back into the company, thereby becoming involved.

When Amstrad launched the first low-cost PC in the UK (priced £500) David Goldman's response was to produce – within six weeks – an accounts package priced £99 to run on the Amstrad. Its launch was the beginning of low-cost software in the UK market, and the business just took off from there.

David was outstanding because he understood marketing. He wasn't hung up about the product *per se*. When people

W hen Amstrad launched the first low-cost PC in the UK... David Goldman's response was to produce – within six weeks – an accounts package priced £99 to run on the Amstrad.

phoned up and asked: 'How do we buy invoices to work with your accounting product?' instead of shrugging his shoulders, he said: 'We'll produce them!' He was a printer, of course, so he produced invoices and payslips. When people asked: 'How do we make this thing work?' meaning not only: 'How do we turn the computer on?' but also 'How do we do the month-end routines? How do we do some of the accounting functions that go with the software package?' Sage gave them the answers. The company began to advise customers and, significantly, began to charge for the information. Back in the early 1980s it was unusual for software companies to charge for their telephone support, but Sage did. Since then, telephone support has become an extremely important part of the Sage business, and a very important reason for people buying and continuing to buy the product.

The bold decision to develop the accounting product became transformational for the business. At a time when the sales turnover was less than £40,000 a month, I remember arriving at the office at 7.30 one morning (the boys didn't get there till

8.30, of course, being good software people) and not being able to get in because my way was blocked by a vast number of mailbags full of orders containing £99 cheques for our new accounting product. It was extraordinary.

He was prepared to invest 50 per cent of the sales revenue of the business back into marketing.

As sales took off, Goldman's entrepreneurial flair and his marketing skills showed again. He was prepared to invest 50 per cent of the sales revenue of the business back into marketing. At the time that was something people just didn't do. Goldman's innovations – charging for support and putting 50 per cent of the sales revenue back into marketing – enabled us to realize almost from day one that we had an opportunity. We realized that if we could establish ourselves as the number one vendor of low-cost accounting software in the market, we would be in a very powerful position. That he achieved his aim was a mark of Goldman's combined entrepreneurial and marketing skills. His rare combination of abilities was, without question, the reason for Sage's success. 🢖🢖

Executive Timeline Michael Jackson

Early years	Degree in law, Cambridge University
	Qualified as an accountant.
	Worked in industry in the UK and USA.
1987–1990	Worked in a small investment bank.
1990	**Elderstreet**
	Founding Director
	A mainly technology-based venture capital firm that invests in the software sector.
	Sold Elderstreet to Dresdner Kleinwort Capital in 2000. Bought it back in 2003.
1993–1994	**Sage Group**
	Deputy Chairman
	Sage is a leading supplier of accounting and business management software to small and medium-sized businesses.
1997–present	*Chairman*

Never have a list that comprises more than four or five things to do at any one time. Concentrating on these few things and making them a high priority is the best form of time management.

7 **Focus on Four or Five Things**
Don Cruickshank

Former Chairman, *London Stock Exchange*

My Career

 I moved into industry in 1967 and worked for Alcan Aluminium. It was a Canadian company with a management style quite different from the style in British industry at that time. After that I became one of the first two non-US MBAs recruited by McKinsey into their London office and spent about five years there. Then came a completely random jump into newspapers. I stayed in the newspaper industry until 1980, when, following my unsuccessful attempt with Harold Evans to lead a management buyout of *The Sunday Times*, Rupert Murdoch bought *The Times* and *The Sunday Times*. That was a good experience. Two further jobs in media followed: the first with Pearson, and then, in 1984, I joined Richard Branson as Managing Director of the Virgin Group, later becoming Managing Director of the Entertainment and Music Group, which became a public company. I also helped Richard with his private businesses, including the airline.

During the same period, at the age of forty-three, I became Chairman of Wandsworth Health Authority in London. That got me involved in the politics of health and healthcare. When Richard brought his companies back into private ownership in 1989, that experience encouraged me to see whether my management skills or lessons learned could be deployed to effect in the National Health Service. I went to Scotland to become Chief Executive of the NHS in Scotland.

While based in Scotland I was headhunted in 1993 by Michael Heseltine to become Director General of Telecoms at Oftel.

I worked there for five years. After that I held two odd jobs: conducting a review of competition in retail banking in the UK for Gordon Brown, the Chancellor of the Exchequer – that was good fun, not least because I spent eighteen months inside HM Treasury – and leading the UK's Y2K campaign.

Following that, as has happened a number of times in my career for reasons I don't properly understand, I was headhunted to be Chairman of the London Stock Exchange. I had no relevant financial services experience, but presumably offered some talent and potential. I achieved what I was asked to achieve and left the role in July 2003. Since then I've been Chairman of Scottish Media Group, Chairman of the publishing company Taylor & Francis, and for the first time have become Chairman of a software company in the private capital world. I took this last role because I wanted to get direct experience of where science and technology is taking us and I'm working with a team of thirty-year-olds, which is very good for me.

Don Cruickshank

Former Chairman, *London Stock Exchange*

There mustn't be a further list of six, seven or fifteen items existing somewhere at the back of your head. You really have to believe that there are only four or five things to be done.

Never focus on more than four or five things at a time. And never make a list that includes more than four or five things to do at once.

This is easier said than done. Quite early in my career I had an opportunity to deal with Rupert Murdoch; I worked for Sir Richard Branson; I even had a brush with Robert Maxwell. These entrepreneurs were extraordinarily successful, but were also blinkered. They had just one or two or a maximum of four or five things that they wanted to get done and see done at any one time. It's important to focus only on this short list; there mustn't be a further list of six, seven or fifteen items existing somewhere at the back of your head. You really have to believe that there are only four or five things to be done.

For someone who is professionally or academically trained, this is actually quite tough to achieve. Narrowing your focus requires self-discipline and practice. It's not just a matter of picking four or five things out of a long list and becoming fixated on them. The short list has to be flexible. It was fascinating, for instance, to watch Richard Branson shifting

Narrowing your focus requires self-discipline and practice.

his priorities. He would slowly drop item number three and introduce a new item. You'd notice that he began to spend less time on the original item number three; then he'd stop talking about it, and a little while later he genuinely wouldn't remember that item had ever been a priority, and something else would have slipped in.

I cannot emphasize enough how important this principle is, whether in negotiation with colleagues or subordinates about objectives and what it is they're trying to achieve, or in the way you allocate your own time. I find it immensely useful. My time management technique is to crystallize the four or five things that I'm meant to be doing and then just work on them. If there are other things to do that I haven't picked up, well, they aren't picked up, but very rarely to anyone's disadvantage I might say.

1967–1970	**Alcan Aluminium**
	Finance, systems and marketing projects work.
	A Canadian aluminium company.
1972–1977	**McKinsey & Co Inc**
	Consultant
	A management consultancy.
1977–1980	**Times Newspapers**
	Commercial Director
1979–1980	***The Sunday Times***
	General Manager
1980–1983	**Pearson plc**
	Managing Director – Finance, Administration, Planning
	Pearson is a media group, which at this time included:
	the *Financial Times*, Goldcrest, Longman and Penguin.
1984–1989	**Virgin Group plc**
	Managing Director
	Managing Director – Entertainment and Music Group
1986–1989	**Wandsworth Health Authority**
	Chairman
1989–1993	**National Health Service, Scotland**
	Chief Executive
1993–1998	**Oftel**
	Director-General – Telecommunications
	Oftel was the the UK's industry regulator.
1997–2000	Led the Y2K campaign, the UK government's
	millennium bug campaign.
1998–2000	**HM Treasury**
	Chairman
	Supervised 'Competition in UK Banking: A Report to
	The Chancellor of the Exchequer', published 2000.
2000–2003	**London Stock Exchange**
	Chairman
2003–2004	**The Scottish Media Group plc**
	Chairman

The prevailing sense of dissatisfaction that greets the successful entrepreneur upon waking every morning is the essential element needed to drive change and improve a business.

8a   **The Essence of the Entrepreneur**
      Lord Kalms

President, *Dixons Group*

My Career

I started my career in 1948 working with my father. We had a couple of shops that quickly reduced to one, and then I started my career with Dixons. It's a career that has been totally focused and based on a very simple philosophy of expanding the business slowly. We floated Dixons in 1962, and from that moment onwards the company has been in continuous growth. Today we have 1400 stores and we trade in thirteen different countries.

Following flotation, I focused on expanding Dixons' inventory and made many small acquisitions. By the middle of the 1980s we had about 300 stores. I then made my biggest acquisition, hard fought, which was to buy Currys, the electrical retail chain.

Taking over Currys was a breakthrough. It put us into the white goods business, and since then it's been a question of consolidating and growing and growing. Today we employ some 35,000 people, which makes it quite a large organization. We've been a FTSE company for a number of years.

During our period of growth, I have concentrated on maintaining high standards, while being very conscious of other interests. We've broadened the base of our social responsibilities, and have been very involved in education. In my own community I have personally funded the building of schools. I try to keep the company focused on social responsibilities as well as wealth creation, and I've achieved that with a modicum of success.

Dixons' City Technology College in Bradford is the apple of my eye, and a wonderful example of how business can relate to, and make a major contribution to, a community. I am passionate about the big role that business should play in a community.

I was given a knighthood in 1996 for services to my industry. I've also been very involved within the political arena. I am passionate about Europe and not giving in to the bureaucracy and the autonomy of Brussels. I fought very strongly to keep the pound against the euro. I founded Business for Sterling in the 1990s, which turned out to be one of the most powerful lobby groups ever and influenced the CBI, which favoured the euro, in its decision to become neutral. The lobby group managed to persuade business that the euro was not good for the UK, and my political involvement continued. I ended up as Treasurer of the Conservative Party – a pretty tough job – and as a result of that I was given a peerage in June 2004. I've been fairly successful and am glad to have been highly regarded. I also have quite a few honorary degrees.

Lord Kalms

President, *Dixons Group*

Change, change, change and a sense of dissatisfaction: those are the major ingredients of successful entrepreneurship.

The entrepreneurial characteristic that everybody needs in business is a sense of continual dissatisfaction. I've been gifted with being totally dissatisfied, and as a result when I wake up each morning I always feel that I've got to achieve more: that I'm not achieving what I want to achieve. It's the sense that nothing should be permanent. Offices should never be permanent. If you walk around your head office, nothing must remain in the same position for long. The entrepreneur is always moving things, changing things, changing people. The sense of dissatisfaction, the demand for change is the spirit of the entrepreneur. The entrepreneur is always looking, seeking other things to do to broaden his range.

In my particular case, the need to expand my range started with selling cameras. I had no conception in those days of the new technologies, but when new technology or a new product came along I sniffed it, and it would be in my store as soon as possible. My store's range had to be bigger, wider, offering more, and always changing. Change, change, change and a sense of dissatisfaction: those are the major ingredients of successful entrepreneurship.

Creating and growing a retail business requires an understanding of where your core business lies, and an obsession with securing a competitive edge.

There's not a single thing that I've learnt over the years that didn't have its seeds in my early days.

In essence, retailing is about having the right ranges, giving customers good service, making sure the customer comes back, catching the customer when he's focusing on buying something, having a philosophy of integrity and ethical behaviour, and having good relationships with your employees. When all is said and done, they are the people who create your business.

There's not a single thing that I've learnt over the years that didn't have its seeds in my early days. I started working with my father in about 1948 in a tiny photographic studio that sold a few cameras and films. It wasn't really a retail business; it was essentially a studio, and the studio business was in its dying phases. So I had to decide where my future would be.

There seemed to be a good demand for cheap cameras, so gradually I expanded the range of what was available. In those post-war days it was very difficult to get merchandise and equipment, but as I slowly built up my ranges, I realized that there was a tremendous demand for photographic equipment, cameras, films and processing. That, really, was the nucleus of the business. After a few months I decided this was it. I could see the future potential, I could *smell* the market and I realized instinctively that it offered an enormous

After a few months I decided this was it. I could see the future potential, I could *smell* the market and I realized instinctively that it offered an enormous opportunity.

opportunity. It became quite clear that I was going to be a mass merchandiser. I found this out simply by trying to sell large quantities of products and seeing that the customers who bought them were not enthusiasts – they just wanted to own a camera. People were becoming more affluent, there were very few cameras on the market and people wanted to buy new toys. These people were my market and my main focus, and gradually I built up a lot of goodwill.

My mass-market focus was brought home to me one Saturday in particular when a rather elderly gentleman came into the shop. He introduced himself as the secretary of the local photographic society and said he wanted to chat to me about technology, filters and processing. He showed me his pictures and he just felt that the store was his base. He also asked me whether I would give a discount to his members. In a flash I said to myself: 'He is not your type of customer. This is not who you want in your shops.' I bid him goodbye rather quickly. He was upset, but as far as I was concerned, I was a mass-merchandiser, not a speciality retailer.

I managed growth by focusing on the essentials. The first thing was to preserve every pound of profit. It's very easy when running a small business to see it as a source of cash flow. However, I realized very quickly that every penny reinvested in the business would give me a much greater return than if I indulged in spending it. I was very mean with what I took out, and every penny went back into the business to buy more stock. I quickly appreciated that the more stock you had, the more volume you would turn over.

I realized very quickly that every penny reinvested in the business would give me a much greater return than if I indulged in spending it.

Expansion in a retail business is comparatively easy. All you need is more shops. I set up a small mail-order business. I realized that there was a big demand throughout the country, and by using the mail-order lists I could identify those parts where there was a particular interest in the product. As far as I was concerned, the first few years were to be used to find new branches. In those days finding new sites was extremely difficult. There was a lot of resistance because I didn't yet have a proven track record. Nevertheless, slowly and one by one I managed to put together half a dozen shops in different parts of the country.

Having achieved my aim, I then asked myself: 'Where next? Should I open more shops? How can I develop a real competitive edge?' In those days there was retail price maintenance, so I wasn't allowed to cut even a penny off the price of any product that I'd bought from a wholesaler, manufacturer or importer. They controlled the price I sold at, and I saw this as my glass ceiling.

There was no way that I could achieve a real competitive edge if I had to sell at the same price as everyone else. Then the opportunity came to travel abroad, to the Far East, and in travelling to Hong Kong, Japan and Korea I felt as if I had discovered El Dorado. I found manufacturers there who would supply me direct under my own brand, even though I was very small, and so I gained complete control of my own retail pricing. That was how I really smashed the glass ceiling.

Executive Timeline Lord Kalms

1937	**Dixons** founded as Dixon Studios Ltd.
1948	Began career working for father.
	Grew Dixons from the one-store family business and turned it into Europe's leading electrical retailer.
1962	Dixons flotation.
Until 1971	*Chief Executive*
1971–2002	**Dixons Group**
	Chairman
1984	Acquisition of Currys
	Currys was the UK's largest electrical retailer.
1996	Awarded a knighthood in recognition of services to the electrical retailing industry.
2002	*Life President*
	Stepped down from the Board to become Life President.
2004	Awarded a life peerage.

Using a prominent person as the public face of a company will personalize a brand and make it easier to gain press coverage. People love human-interest stories; manufacturing a rivalry with a competitor is an ideal way to draw media attention.

9a **Building Brand Awareness**
Stelios Haji-Ioannou

Founder and Chairman, *easyGroup*

My Career

" My name is Stelios; everybody calls me Stelios rather than using my surname. I was born into a Greek shipping family, so I come from an affluent background. I was raised in Athens and came to London twenty years ago to go to university at the London School of Economics and City University Business School. I worked for my father for about four years after graduating, and although I learnt a lot from him, I hated every minute of it. I knew very early on that I wanted to be my own boss.

I started a string of entrepreneurial ventures, the oldest of which is called Stelmar, now twelve years old, a shipping company listed on the New York stock exchange. My second venture (the first to be branded 'easy') was the airline easyJet, which I started about ten years ago. Since then, I have moved into my third phase as an entrepreneur, focusing on extending the brand. I consider myself now to be more of a brand manager than a shipping magnate or an airline owner, and I'm in the process of extending into a dozen different sectors. I've had my fair share of failures and successes, but so far every single one of my companies is still in existence, and most of the older ones are profitable. I am determined to keep extending the brand until I paint the world orange.

Stelios Haji-Ioannou

Founder and Chairman, *easyGroup*

Building Brand Awareness

The cheapest and quickest way to build a brand without having access to a large advertising budget is to use someone as the public face of the company. People are interested in human-interest stories, so newspapers and media tend generally to talk about people rather than companies. If they run a story about the person who spearheads the brand, the resulting publicity is bound to be an easy way to brand-build. The ideal method is to choose an enemy, a company (preferably a household name) that you can pick a fight with.

Nobody had heard of easyJet when I started the company in 1995: it was an uphill struggle for the first couple of years. Then British Airways (BA) decided to enter the market, picking a fight with us by creating Go (a company that easyJet plc subsequently bought). It was very convenient to encourage the story in the media that easyJet was so successful and making such a difference in the aviation market that even British Airways, 'the world's favourite airline', had to imitate it. The fact that I was personally present on the first flight of Go wearing an orange jumpsuit also did its part to hijack the media opportunity in our favour.

We were not the only low-cost airline back then; we co-existed with companies such as Ryanair, which is still around, and Debonair, which is not. I believe it was our ability to grab the opportunity to be seen by the public as the arch-rival of BA that elevated easyJet above the other low-cost airlines, thereby making easyJet a household name in Britain within a couple of years.

A new company needs an entrepreneurial culture and a strong leader to succeed, but if it is to grow into a profitable plc, entrepreneurial drive and flexibility have to be balanced against the need to limit risk and safeguard reliability.

9b   **Balancing Entrepreneurial and plc Cultures**

Very, very few people of an entrepreneurial nature make it all the way to leading a major plc.

The only way to start a company is to have a strong entrepreneurial culture led usually by a single individual. However, very, very few people of an entrepreneurial nature make it all the way to leading a major plc. At some stage in the company's evolution more process-orientated professional managers need to be brought into the team to strike the balance between risk management and entrepreneurial drive.

I created easyJet in 1995. Since then I have overseen the evolution of the company from its early entrepreneurial stages (when it was touch-and-go as to whether it would survive), through profitability and success within a five-year timeframe, to flotation in 2000 and the present day. It is now a fairly large company with a turnover in excess of £1 billion. As the founder, I have now stepped aside and allow professional management to run the company on a day-to-day basis, despite the fact that I retain a significant shareholding.

I observed the culture change as the company grew from being an entrepreneurial start-up to becoming a plc; the transformation is one of the most amazing that can be seen in business. Some companies do it well and some do it less well: some things are easier after becoming a plc and some things are worse. For example, if you have two aircraft and one of the

I observed the culture change as the company grew from being an entrepreneurial start-up to becoming a plc; the transformation is one of the most amazing that can be seen in business.

two is grounded because it has a technical fault, you are in deep trouble. No matter how many entrepreneurs you have on hand to help and to apologize to customers, as I used to, you're in deep trouble because 50 per cent of your customers are disappointed. If you have in the region of 100 aircraft – as easyJet does now – and one of them is grounded for a technical fault, nobody notices.

From the point of view of customer/consumer benefit, a bigger company sometimes offers a more reliable service as there's more expertise employed in the company, and the skill set is spread across many individuals rather than it being a one-man show. At the same time, the company becomes less flexible, less capable of changing and less agile. The risk is that in five or ten years' time another entrepreneur, another Stelios, will come up with a new business model, or the latest concept in aviation, and will bring the plc into difficulties.

There is always a fine balance to be achieved in a plc between maintaining your entrepreneurial nature in order to evolve and limiting the level of risk you take because you're managing other people's money. Shareholders are typically hands-off, very risk-averse and don't really like other people gambling with their money. I'm not sure I'm an expert in striking the balance: my heart and soul are those of an entrepreneur. Being an entrepreneur is what I'm good at, it's what I've been for years and I've now started twelve companies.

A bigger company... becomes less flexible, less capable of changing and less agile.

When a business becomes a plc it needs to introduce more people: professional management who are more risk-averse, more process-orientated and who will counterbalance the entrepreneurial drive. The risk is that the processes may start to dominate and the company may suffer as a result. The high street is full of names that were glorious in the past and have now fallen by the wayside. Success and progress mean a never-ending struggle between the two tensions. 99

Executive Timeline Stelios Haji-Ioannou

1987	Degree in economics, London School of Economics
1988	MSc in Shipping Trade and Finance, City University Business School, London
	Troodos Shipping Worked for his father.
1992	**CYMEPA** (Cyprus Marine Environment Protection Association) *Founding Chairman*
	Stelmar Tankers *Founding Director* First venture in the shipping industry.
1995	**easyJet** *Founding Director* A low-cost, no-frills, point-to-point airline.
1998	**easyGroup** Formed as a holding company to explore new ventures to extend the 'easy' brand and capitalize upon the expanding use of the Internet.
1999	**easyInternetcafé** started trading.
2000	**easyJet** listed on the London stock exchange.
	easyCar, easyValue.com, easy.com started trading.
2001	**Stelmar** listed on the New York stock exchange.
	easyMoney started trading.
2003	**easyCinema** started trading.
2004	**easyBus, easyPizza, easyJobs, easy4men** started trading.
	Stelmar sold to NYSE-listed shipping company OSG.
2005	**easyMobile, easyCruise, easyHotel** started trading.

It's important in
business to be ambitious
and aim high. Like
life, business is about
growth and progress, so
be ambitious early on as
life is too short for small
ideas.

10a **Aim Big, Then Deliver**
Luke Johnson

Chairman, *Signature Restaurants*, and Chairman, *Channel 4 Television*

My Career

I first became involved in business while I was at university running clubs for students. After I left university I became a stockbroker. I went out on my own in the late 1980s and undertook various ventures such as classic cars and theatre scenery. In 1992 I got involved in the purchase of Pizza Express, and from 1993 to 1999 I worked with a team of partners to grow the business from about twelve company-owned restaurants to nearer 250. I became Chairman of the company during that period.

I also got involved in a number of other companies, including a restaurant business called My Kinda Town that was sold to Capital Radio, and a port business that we sold to Associated British Ports for £100 million. Since 1999 I've built up another restaurant group called Signature; it includes Strada – a chain of twenty-five wood-fired pizzerias – and we also own places such as The Ivy and the Belgo Group. I am the principal owner. During the same period I also built up the UK's largest chain of dentists – Integrated Dental Holdings – which, with my two business partners, I have just taken private. Early in 2004 I became Chairman of Channel 4.

Luke Johnson

Chairman, *Signature Restaurants*, and Chairman, *Channel 4 Television*

Aim Big, Then Deliver

It's important to take the attitude that the concept is never going to be quite 100 per cent and that things can always be done better.

It's important to me to be ambitious and to aim big in business. Sometimes in the past I was not ambitious enough, and as a result I keep trying to push myself harder to be more ambitious. As an example, four years ago we started Strada, our chain of wood-fired pizzerias. We began with the idea that we would make it a big chain rather than just an individual, perfectly formed restaurant. From the outset we were working out what would appeal and what we could replicate rather than focusing on a simple, unique location. I'm forever pushing my business partners to be more ambitious and to take on more sites. As long as they're in a good location, we'll find the money, we will find the right people to employ, and the customers will come.

It's important to take the attitude that the concept is never going to be quite 100 per cent and that things can always be done better; we are forever trying to refine the concept and perfect it. In the meantime, the new openings are being successful. We aim to have a national business, and in four years we've opened twenty-five restaurants. So far, things are going well.

Striking a balance between aiming big and dealing with the day-to-day activity is always a challenge. We tend to deal with matters as they come up on a weekly basis: should we hire a new chef, or should we stick with the chef we've got, who costs less but perhaps isn't as imaginative? Should we use suppliers who are more geared up to supply restaurants? Should we adopt a more expensive software system that can cope with multiple units? Decisions about matters of detail are an everyday occurrence, and in one sense it can be useful to have limited capital so that it acts as a constraint: you can spend only what you've got. However, there are numerous businesses that go through painful growing pains because they aren't ambitious at an early enough stage in their choice of premises, in taking out patents or in dealing with their IT hiccups. If you are ambitious, you should always take on people who are slightly better than you can afford, and choose space that gives you slightly more room than you need because then you can grow into it. Allowing room for development is a good thing because business and life are about growth and progress, and you've got to aim high.

The secret of business success is to turn a good idea into a thriving business. It is a common error to assume that having the idea is what matters. Everyone has ideas: it's the translation of those ideas into action that makes the difference. Putting an idea into action is difficult and boring,

If you are ambitious you should always take on people who are slightly better than you can afford, and choose space that gives you slightly more room than you need because then you can grow into it.

and generally takes a lot longer and costs more than one would like. Progress is fraught with setbacks and blind alleys, but that's what makes the difference. If I could have £1000 for every new restaurant concept that someone has put to me, I'd be a lot wealthier than I am. Coming up with concepts is easy. The reality of business is in the hard graft of recruiting people, finding suppliers, finding a site, fitting it out, dealing with the health and safety officers, the environmental officers, the planners and all the rest of it, funding the thing, coping with the start-up losses, and dealing with customers day in, day out. Those things are the reality of business. The big ideas are cheap.

The big wins are the deals that matter. Mistakes and setbacks are inevitable, but don't let them depress you or pull you off course. Keep pressing on, as these things are unimportant once you find a big winner.

10b   **The Big Win Outweighs the Setbacks**

The Big Win Outweighs the Setbacks

Business life is about searching for major wins because they matter much more than the setbacks and the failures.

Over the years it has become my belief that it's the big wins that matter. Mistakes and setbacks are inevitable and you should not let them depress you or pull you off course.

I learnt this lesson most strongly in 1992. I'd been self-employed for about three years and had struggled through the recession with a number of projects that didn't really work. To my mind I had made very little progress. In the late summer of 1992 an opportunity arose to buy control of Pizza Express. My partners and I had been pursuing the company as a target for a couple of years, but there had been no prospect of purchase until that time. We spent the rest of that year focused intently on seeing off the competition and raising the funding. We succeeded in early 1993, and had the benefit of immediate success from that undertaking. Our timing was fortuitous because 1993 marked the beginning of the end of the recession, or the start of the upturn in the economy – but, more important, we gained control of a great brand and a tremendous business. Suddenly the failures and pressures of the previous two or three years melted into insignificance. The simple lesson is that if you invest £1 in each of two businesses, you can lose only £1 in each, but if the business succeeds, you can make a multiple of many times £1. That's a great lesson. As long as you don't do something foolish, such as giving a personal guarantee, you can lose only what you risk. In a successful business, on the other hand, the upside is unlimited.

Balancing the setbacks and slow progress against the big wins is not easy, but it's the type of thing that becomes easier to handle if you have a team around you. Over the last ten years I've put most of my energy into what I see as the critical areas for growth within the businesses I've been involved with. Be ambitious, take bold steps, weigh up the really critical areas and don't get too bogged down in detail. Although the detail certainly does matter, it's the major decisions as to whether or not to invest in that new factory or whether to make that acquisition that will really turn the business around, and transform it from being a small business into a big one.

Often it will be two or three years before you can really tell whether or not a business is a winner. Deciding whether to keep plugging away at something or to give up is the real test of genius. I've certainly committed errors by not plugging away at a particular project and by switching my attention or selling out too early. On the other hand, I've also plugged away for too long at something that is doomed, thereby wasting a lot of time and money. These mistakes are ones we make over and over again, but if you keep going and if you've got the energy, I suspect that sooner or later you'll hit payday.

Deciding whether to keep plugging away at something or to give up is the real test of genius.

Business life is about searching for major wins because they matter much more than the setbacks and the failures. One big win can cancel out half a dozen small disasters. **"**

Executive Timeline Luke Johnson

Early career	Oxford University
	Ran club nights whilst studying medicine.
	BMP
	BMP is an advertising agency
	Kleinwort Benson
	Media analyst
	Kleinwort Benson is an investment bank.
1992	Led a takeover bid for the Pizza Express restaurant chain.
1993–1999	**Pizza Express**
	Chairman
1999–present	**Signature Restaurants**
	Chairman
	The Signature chain includes Strada, The Ivy and the Belgo Group.
	Integrated Dental Holdings
	Integrated Dental Holdings is the UK's largest owner of dental practices.
2004–present	**Channel 4 Television**
	Chairman
	Channel 4 is a commercially funded broadcaster and publisher.

There is no substitute for experience – learn more from the best minds in business

Did you know that Fifty Lessons has created a must-have digital library containing more than 350 *filmed* business lessons that can be viewed online, from home or in your office?

Through Fifty Lessons you can:

- Experience first-hand the real-life learning of some of the most influential business leaders of our time.
- Gain access to a vast array of concise lessons covering over thirty-five key leadership and management topics.
- Benefit from decades of hard-won learning and experience.

To subscribe to Fifty Lessons, and to take advantage of our special reader discount, please visit www.fiftylessons.com/readeroffer for details.

We also offer customized solutions for larger organizations, from providing lessons on DVD and print to distributing tailored lesson packages via email and corporate intranets. For further information please visit www.fiftylessons.com or

For corporate sales enquiries please contact:

BBC Worldwide Learning
Woodlands
80 Wood Lane
London
W12 0TT
United Kingdom
Tel: +44 (0)20 8433 1641
Fax: +44 (0)20 8433 2916
Email:
corporate.sales @bbc.co.uk

For any other enquiries please contact:

Fifty Lessons
Fitzroy House
11 Chenies Street
London
WC1E 7EY
United Kingdom
Tel: +44 (0)20 7636 4777
Fax: +44 (0)20 7636 4888
Email:
info@fiftylessons.com